31 Reasons
To Stay Alive

A Guided Journal For an Amazing Person Who Doesn't Always Know How Amazing They Are

Disclaimer

This journal is not intended to replace professional, mental care. It is not a means to diagnose, treat, cure, or heal any physical or mental medical conditions. Please consult a licensed professional for care concerning medical or emotional matters.

In the event that you or someone you know feels that life is no longer worth living, please call or text 988.

You Are NOT Alone

This journal was designed and created by someone with depression and anxiety who has been where you are. Ms. James and all of us at Ametrine Publishing value YOU as the wonderful individual that you are.

We at Ametrine Publishing want you to know that you matter and that the world would be an absolutely terrible place without you in it.

One Month Contract

I,_____, promise to give myself at LEAST one full month from today to give myself the opportunity to live life to its fullest potential and to seek outside help from a friend, therapist, or doctor if I feel that it is becoming too difficult for me to honor this agreement at any time and for any reason. I will renew this contract with myself in one month's time.

Signed this _____ day of _____, 20__

_____
Signature

Even if you feel completely alone, know that your tribe is out there and they can't wait to meet you.

Day 1

My ideal tribe of people is...

_____

_____

_____

_____

_____

_____

_____

My affirmation for today is: "I have the authority to choose who I want in my life and who I do not.."

Kindness is the engine that moves humanity forward

Day 2

These are the ways that I was kind to myself today...

Be Kind To Yourself

_____

_____

_____

_____

_____

_____

_____

_____

My affirmation for today is: "I deserve to be loved by me"

It's never too late
to be who you
might have been
~ George Eliot

Day 3

These are some things I have always wanted to try...

_____

_____

_____

_____

_____

_____

_____

_____

My affirmation for today is: "If Colonel Sanders could start over and become successful in his 60s, I can start my new goals today"

TOMORROW

is

ANOTHER DAY

~ Margaret Mitchell
Gone With The Wind

Day 4

Here are at least 3 things that I thought would never get better, but they did...

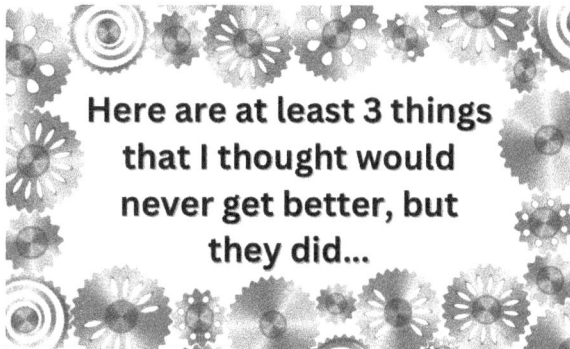

I'm a
HUSTLER
Baby

_____

_____

_____

_____

_____

_____

_____

My affirmation for today is: "This too shall pass" ~ Everyone's grandmother. Ever.

Day 5

Here is a list of
things I used to wish
for myself that are
now my reality...

THE BEST
is yet
To Be

_____

_____

_____

_____

_____

_____

_____

My affirmation for today is: "A younger version of me once wished to be where I am today, and I know the future will bring more opportunities for me to be what I now wish to be"

I Am Safe Even When I Make a Mistake

Day 6

This is how I will give myself a second chance today...

DON't
QUIT

_____

_____

_____

_____

_____

_____

_____

_____

My affirmation for today is: "I support myself and I encourage myself to try again as many times as I need to."

Day 7

Here is where I went to get some sunlight today...

_____

_____

_____

_____

_____

_____

_____

_____

My affirmation for today is: "Plants require sunlight to thrive and so do I."

My furry friend counts on me

Day 8

Here is how I spent quality time with my pet today...

_____

_____

_____

_____

_____

_____

_____

_____

My affirmation for today is: "The unconditional love of my pet gets me through some rough days"

The Pendulum Will Always Swing Back In My Favor

Day 9

If I wrote my own story, here is how the happy ending would look...

Keep
Going

_____

_____

_____

_____

_____

_____

_____

_____

My affirmation for today is: "Things rarely stay the way they are, so change for the better is inevitable"

HOLD

ON

Day 10

These are articles or videos that gave me motivation today...

You can't

_____
_____
_____
_____
_____
_____
_____
_____

My affirmation for today is: "I am stronger than anything that has been designed to break me."

TRUST
* *the* *
# PROCESS

Day 11

Here are a few small things that I believe I can accomplish...

Believe

_____

_____

_____

_____

_____

_____

_____

_____

My affirmation for today is: "I believe in myself and I believe that things are working out for me even when I am not sure how yet."

Day 12

Here is how I felt after focusing solely on my breathing for 10 minutes..

_____
_____
_____
_____
_____
_____
_____

My affirmation for today is: "I realize that the simple act of breathing is a miracle and I will focus closely on my breathing today."

Day 13

Here is how I felt after focusing solely on my breathing for 15 minutes..

breathe

_____

_____

_____

_____

_____

_____

_____

My affirmation for today is: "My lungs are telling me to go on, so I shall go on."

Day 14

Here is how I felt after focusing solely on my breathing for 30 minutes..

_____
_____
_____
_____
_____
_____
_____
_____

My affirmation for today is: "Today is an opportunity to do something I didn't do yesterday."

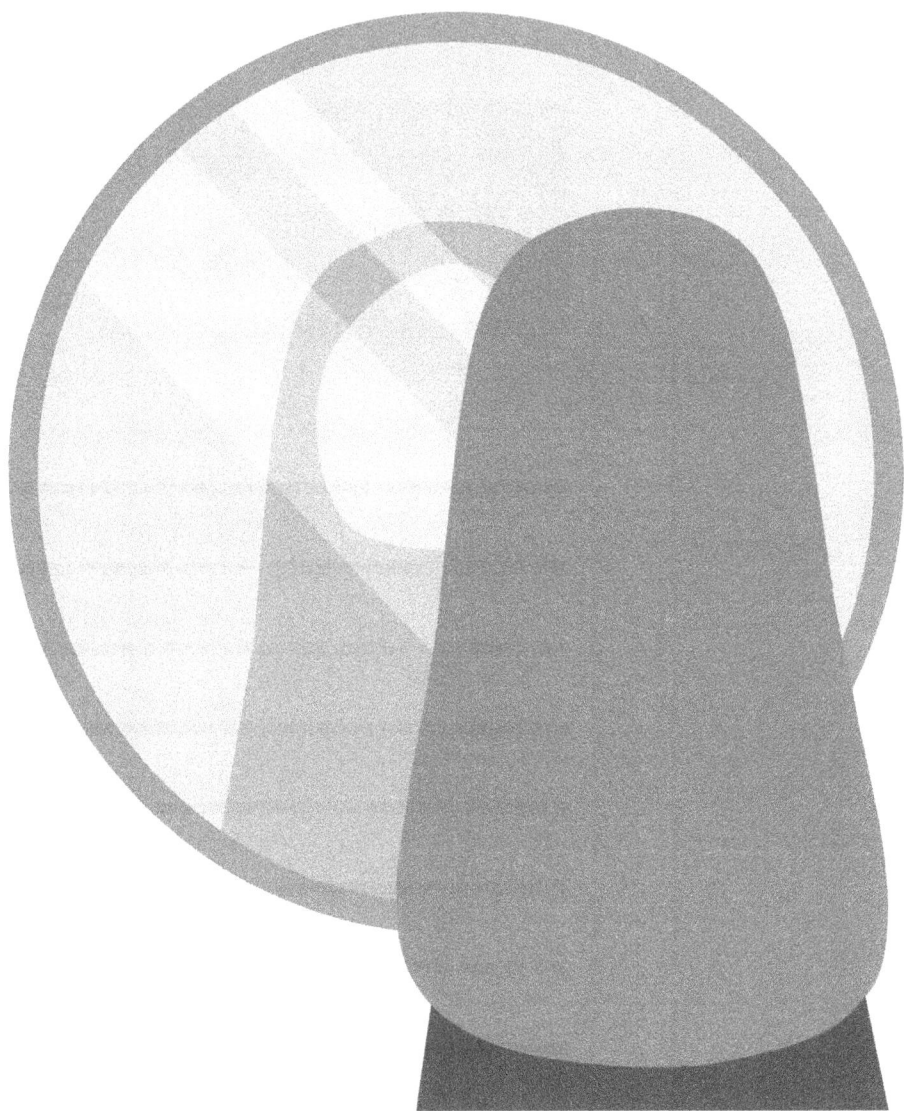

Day 15

Here is what I told myself in the mirror today...

_____

_____

_____

_____

_____

_____

_____

_____

My affirmation for today is: "I will speak kindly to myself and of myself today because I know that words have power."

$Day 16$

Here is what I told myself in the mirror today...

_____

_____

_____

_____

_____

_____

_____

_____

My affirmation for today is: "I am good enough just the way I am."

Day 17

Here is what I told myself in the mirror today...

_____

_____

_____

_____

_____

_____

_____

_____

My affirmation for today is: "I am wonderfully made and my higher power made NO mistakes in creating me."

Day 18

This is where I went to find a book today and what I found...

Books

Bookstore

Dollar Store

Library

Online

_____

_____

_____

_____

_____

_____

_____

_____

My affirmation for today is: "My thoughts are a reflection of what I feed my mind."

Day 19

This is my favorite book genre and why...

_____

_____

_____

_____

_____

_____

_____

_____

My affirmation for today is: "I can escape whenever I like by reading a great book."

Day 20

This is how I was inspired by what I have been reading...

_____

_____

_____

_____

_____

_____

_____

_____

My affirmation for today is: "I can rewrite my own story whenever I choose."

Day 21

My super power is...

_____

_____

_____

_____

_____

_____

_____

_____

My affirmation for today is: "I am better at being me than anyone else in the world. There is no competition."

If I never existed, my
family would not ...

_____

_____

_____

_____

_____

_____

_____

My affirmation for today is: "I have just as much value as
everyone else in my life."

If I never existed, my community would not …

_____

_____

_____

_____

_____

_____

_____

My affirmation for today is: "I have just as much value as everyone else in my life."

Day 24

If I never existed, my
friends would not …

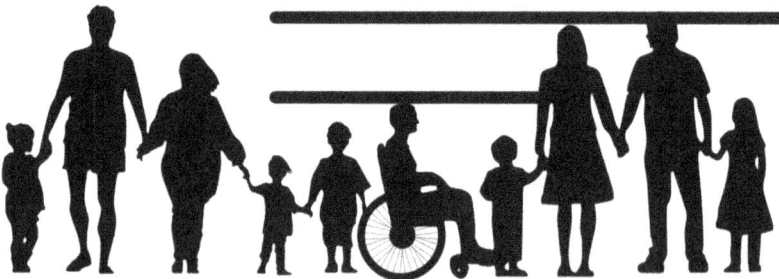

_____
_____
_____
_____
_____
_____
_____

My affirmation for today is: "I have just as much value as
everyone else in my life."

Day 25

If I never existed, people would miss out on ...

_____

_____

_____

_____

_____

_____

_____

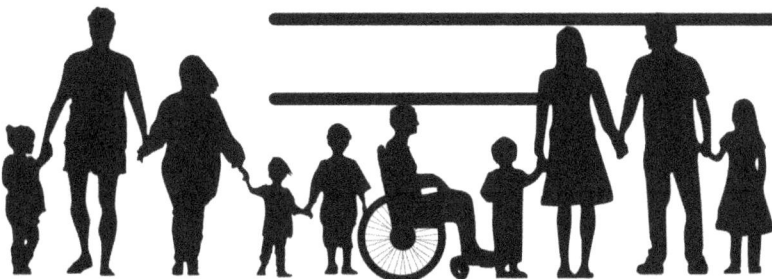

My affirmation for today is: "I have just as much value as everyone else in my life."

Day 26

I cannot leave this world before I visit ...

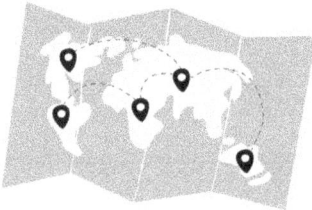

_____

_____

_____

_____

_____

_____

_____

_____

My affirmation for today is: "The world is bigger and more amazing than what I have seen so far."

Day 27

I cannot leave this world before I see...

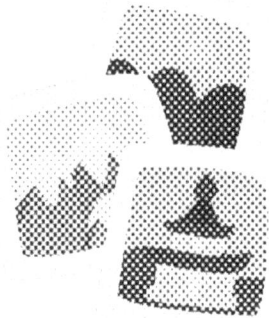

My affirmation for today is: "There is always something incredible to experience."

Day 28

I cannot leave this world before I taste...

_____

_____

_____

_____

_____

_____

_____

_____

My affirmation for today is: "I am going to treat myself to something I've always wanted to eat."

Day 29

I cannot leave this world before I say...

_____

_____

_____

_____

_____

_____

_____

_____

My affirmation for today is: "My thoughts, feelings, and opinions are valid and worth hearing.."

I had a whole concert in the shower today and this is what I sang...

_____

_____

_____

_____

_____

_____

_____

_____

My affirmation for today is: "It feels good to let loose and sing for no one to hear, but me.."

These are ways that I made myself laugh today...

_____
_____
_____
_____
_____
_____
_____
_____

My affirmation for today is: "My joy is mine to give myself."